M000220200

LOVE N

FOR BEX FITZSIMONS

Hardie Grant

BOOKS

MATCH

AN ASTROLOGICAL GUIDE TO LOVE & DATING

STELLA ANDROMEDA

INTRODUCTION P.7

Aries

p. 9

21 MARCH–20 APRIL

Cancer

p. 51

21 JUNE–21 JULY

Taurus

p. 23

21 APRIL–20 MAY

Leo

p. 65

22 JULY–21 AUGUST

Gemini

p. 37

21 MAY–20 JUNE

Virgo

p. 79

22 AUGUST–21 SEPTEMBER

p. 93

Libra

22 SEPTEMBER–21 OCTOBER

p. 135

Capricorn

22 DECEMBER–20 JANUARY

p. 107

Scorpio

22 OCTOBER–21 NOVEMBER

p. 149

Aquarius

21 JANUARY–19 FEBRUARY

p. 121

Sagittarius

22 NOVEMBER–21 DECEMBER

p. 163

Pisces

20 FEBRUARY–20 MARCH

Introduction

Is it written in the stars, or can we utilise the energies of our zodiac signs to our advantage when it comes to love? Knowing your own sun sign characteristics and how they might chafe or chime with those of others can help in the navigation of love's changing seas. And while it can't provide every answer, a basic understanding of astrological influences can help you identify your own characteristics and respond to those of others.

Sometimes it's obvious from the word go what potential or tensions might arise between two lovers, but how you handle these can be helped by a knowledge of the more subtle astrological inclinations. You think he's stubborn, he thinks you're impulsive; but if you know why these energies might clash, there might be an easier way to manage them.

Additional knowledge can also be gleaned from a birth chart (which is easy to do online if you know your, or their, time of birth) and which provides information about the ascendant and moon signs, all key in our understanding of particular traits. So if you also know in which zodiac sign the ascendant and moon fall, reading up on these characteristics too provides even more information with which to work.

In any event, remember that many relationships thrive where there is an element of tension, that little frisson that brings you together in the first place. It all depends on your personal, astrological inclinations, and knowing these can help when making dating choices and negotiating what appeals, and what doesn't.

When it comes to finding harmony in a love match, information about how we respond and react can help. Here, astrology can add insight and excitement, helping us work out how to appreciate our partner, and how to be sure that they appreciate us. That's when the wisdom of the stars is your ally and friend.

Aries

★

The ram

21 MARCH–20 APRIL

Astrologically the first sign of
the zodiac, Aries appears alongside
the vernal (or spring) equinox.
A cardinal fire sign, depicted by
the ram, it is the sign of beginnings
and ruled by planet Mars, which
represents a dynamic ability to
meet challenges energetically
and creatively.

OPPOSITE SIGN

Libra

How does Aries want to be loved?

Because they tend to say what they want, rather than expecting someone to second guess, a lover will have no trouble knowing how Aries wants to be loved. Not given to coy flirtations, Aries tends to take things rather literally and, in return, can find too much subtlety confusing. They operate on a 'what you see is what you get' basis, which can be too much for those who find straightforward expression too demanding, frightening off gentler souls.

Loyalty is very big on the Aries agenda, too, and once they've given their heart, they expect this to be fully reciprocated and, if not, their disappointment may lead to a swift termination of the relationship. Aries may be prepared to give their lover a second chance if they let them down, but seldom a third. The only consideration, however, is that for all their desire for straight-talking and commitment, Aries does like a challenge. So what Aries really wants is the security of commitment with the frisson of a little unpredictability to challenge their status quo.

The bottom line? For as long as Aries is in a relationship they are committed to, they will want complete loyalty and adoration, even if they don't need to be physically close 100 per cent of the time. Their inclination is always to trust, until circumstances or their intuition tells them otherwise, then they will be wary or abruptly cut any ties. Aries expects an immediate response when they text or call, much as a young child demands attention, but for all these inclinations, they will reward like with like, making Aries one of the easiest Sun signs to love.

Where should you take Aries on a mini-break?

With a preference for heat and adventure, Aries aren't often pleased to just lie around on the beach and would prefer to be taken on an exploration of old Marseilles or the Acropolis in Athens, a trek in Ladakh or a yoga retreat in Santa Fe.

What is Aries
like in bed?

Sex for Aries is a straightforward affair and can be quite separate from a need to be loved. That's not to say Aries is promiscuous, but they acknowledge that sex can be enjoyed for its own sake, either with a life partner, committed lover, a good friend or even a fleeting affair. Your body is your ally for Aries, who tends not to shy away from their physical selves, whatever their body type. They may not want the bedroom to be floodlit, but they like to see and respond to their partner, enjoying their pleasure as much as their own.

Confident about getting their sexual needs met, Aries can sometimes seem a little too demanding or dominant for more reticent types. This sexual energy is often apparent in the way they move and communicate outside the bedroom, exuding a sort of physical confidence that can be very attractive. Adventurous Aries doesn't tend to be sexually predictable either: sex toys may be part of their repertoire, and any partner shouldn't be surprised by a bit of playfulness and role-play in the bedroom.

Moving in
with Aries

One of the most generally straightforward of the Sun signs,
Aries' tendency to say what they think and feel can be a benefit in
negotiating domestic relationships – although more sensitive types
may just find them plain tactless. Aries seldom asks others to do
something they're not prepared to do themselves, but it does mean
they like things done their own way. And because they are prone to
impatience, they'll often do the washing up, for example, because
it's quicker than waiting for their other half to get around to it.
The good side? They won't often hold a grudge about it.

The Aries approach to organisation can be a bit slapdash,
which may irritate more precise partners, and their bursts of energy
mean they can get a lot done in a short time – but only for as long as
their attention span is held. This slightly whirlwind approach can
be tricky for more peaceable or pedantic souls, while the Aries lack
of sentimentality might find them throwing out what they see as
clutter, but is in fact their lover's prized possession. This can cause
friction so it is better for Aries to take a moment to ask, first, just
to be sure.

Breaking up
with Aries

Because Aries is such a loyal lover, even if they've been the one to instigate the break-up, they may find it hard to fully let go and will often go to some lengths to maintain a friendship, finding it difficult to understand why an ex may never want to see them again. If Aries is the one rejected, they are hurt and often surprised, and will often push to know and understand why, even if the truth hurts even more. But Aries, generally, doesn't hold a grudge, because basically they know that if they've loved and been loved before, they can love again. Aries is by nature an optimist and believes it's just a matter of time before the next great love affair appears on their horizon.

Aries and . . .

♈

Aries

This can be a passionate union, although with two headstrong egos there may be some jostling for first position. This combination works best when there is room for some mutual independence in career or social life.

♉

Taurus

Steady earth sign Taurus is attracted to Aries' fire, but may find their independence hard to handle. Aries in turn may take their time to appreciate Taurus' dependability, so this pairing requires a bit of give and take.

♊

Gemini

Air can oxygenate fire, so there is an immediate compatibility between Aries' dynamism and Gemini's ingenuity. And because they both love to talk, they may compete for attention, but will never bore each other.

♋

Cancer

The sexual attraction between this fire and water sign combination can be steamy, but Aries may find Cancer's tendency towards defensiveness inhibiting, while the crab's liking for domesticity can fuel Aries' desire for escape.

♌

Leo

Two fiery, open-hearted signs can make a good match, as long as there is some mutual accommodation for their individual egos. Keeping it playful helps, while a generous dose of admiration on both sides makes everyone happy.

♍

Virgo

Not an easy combination because Aries can find Virgo's orderliness restrictive, while Virgo can be suspicious of Aries' spontaneity. If this is kept in mind, however, then much can be gained from the positivity of each other's qualities.

♈ Aries

♎︎

Libra

Libra's peaceful and diplomatic attitude may find Aries' desire for action and confrontation tricky, but Libra's airiness can fan Aries' flame, creating a powerful and unconventional attraction in the short, if not the long, term.

♑︎

Capricorn

Aries may be just a tad unconventional for practical, earthy Capricorn, but there's real strength to be gained for fiery Aries in this grounding relationship with its potential for both mutual respect and sensual commitment.

♏︎

Scorpio

Scorpio's tendency towards possessiveness may dampen Aries' free-spirited ardour, but the chemistry here is a powerful one, as there is an appreciable physical compatibility, which can work well if rooted in mutual intellectual appreciation.

♒︎

Aquarius

Both signs can appreciate each other's need for independence, which can bode well for good compatibility, although Aquarius' airiness may sometimes feel a little too unpredictable even for spontaneous Aries.

♐︎

Sagittarius

As temperamental matches go, these two fire signs are highly compatible and if they can make it work in the bedroom, it's a relationship pretty likely to work anywhere as both tend towards optimism, spontaneity and frankness.

♓︎

Pisces

With a little tact on Aries' part, this can be a fruitful relationship, with Pisces gaining from a robust counterpart to their dreamy, approach to life, which in turn can be very seductive to the less subtle Aries.

Aries

Aries love-o-meter

Least compatible

Virgo   Cancer   Aries   Taurus   Aquarius   Libra

Most compatible

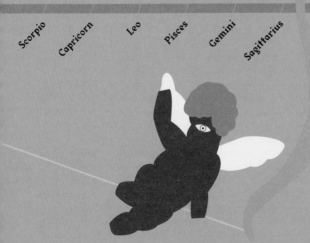

Scorpio Capricorn Leo Pisces Gemini Sagittarius

Taurus

*

The bull

21 APRIL–20 MAY

Grounded, sensual and appreciative
of bodily pleasures, Taurus is a fixed
earth sign endowed by its ruling
planet Venus with grace and a love
of beauty, despite its depiction as
a bull. Generally characterised by
an easy and uncomplicated,
if occasionally stubborn,
approach to life.

OPPOSITE SIGN

Scorpio

How does Taurus want to be loved?

Taurus wants to be loved often and well, with a lot of hugs in between. They like physical acknowledgement that they are cared for, so not for them the airy declarations of love – they want proof and that proof must lie in something tangible. This could be cooking a meal, which they'll appreciate because it's also how they like to show their love and appreciation. Or creating them something lovely for the home (as long as it reflects their taste), but it's not enough just to be told they're loved, Taurus will always seek evidence. The downside is that this can feel quite needy to more independent souls, but once reassured, Taurus is happy. It's a bit of a conundrum, though, because their tendency to be reserved can make Taurus' own declarations of love few and far between. Despite this, still waters run deep and they are, more often than not, trustworthy friends and lovers. Extra-marital affairs aren't Taurus' style either, because their innate tendency to put down roots, combined with an element of laziness, makes them unlikely to stray. 'Why eat burgers out, when you can have steak at home?' might well have been said by a Taurus.

Because the throat is ruled by Taurus, many find their neck a particularly erogenous zone, and a neck and shoulder massage is sure to calm any stress that can arise from overwork. This sort of hands-on bodywork is, generally, a component of how Taurus wants to be loved. They are comfortable with their bodies and love to be massaged, preferably with essential oils in a beautiful location. It's a sure-fire way to calm a raging bull.

What day of the week should you call Taurus?

Friday. The end of the working week for most of us, when the hard-working bull can look forward to some rest. Friday actually links the Old English goddess Frigg with her Roman counterpart, Venus, and we also see this in the French word for Friday, Vendredi.

What is Taurus
like in bed?

Because they are so much about the body, making love is first and foremost a physical connection for sensual Taurus and their foreplay tends towards the straightforward, with lots of eye contact. That physical connection is generally rooted in authenticity and trust, however, so is unlikely to be a one-night stand. Sex will probably have been anticipated and planned for in terms of a comfortable location, as Taurus is unlikely to be spontaneously overwhelmed by lust, which is just too unpredictable to feel comfortable. There can sometimes be an erotic delicacy to Taurean women, which also enhances their sensual style.

Once comfortable, Taurus can be playful, even earthy and bawdy in that Chaucerian way. As long as the trust is there, they are up for suggestions to explore new sexual territory and even role play, but only up to a point, as too much fantasy isn't a turn-on. What is really relished is that deep post-sex security: Taurus is very happy to sleep in another's arms. In fact, they often consider sex the best sleep aid there is.

Moving in
with Taurus

A desire for beautiful surroundings alongside a practical streak
means that daily chores get done, the bathroom cabinet only
contains what's needed and the washing up tends to be done every
night, in an effort to create the calm, secure ambience that lies close
to a Taurean heart. The Taurus home also tends to contain the best
their budget can afford, whether it's sumptuous bath towels or a
state-of-the-art kitchen spatula.

Taurus is considered one of the easier signs to live with, but
only as long as things are going their way, which can require a bit
of compromise as standing up to the bull can be tricky. Because
Taurus has a love and appreciation of beautiful possessions, they
can be very possessive, not necessarily great on sharing, and won't
take kindly to having their stuff borrowed without permission (if
at all!). But Taurus is known for their generosity in other ways, and
they like their home to be comfortable and welcoming to guests,
are hospitable and generous hosts, just as long as everyone
remembers to wipe their feet on their way in.

Breaking up
with Taurus

Break-ups are difficult for Taurus because they seldom commit unless they're 100 per cent sure and in it for the long haul. Any break-up is also hard because it presents a major change, and it may take Taurus a while to commit again having believed this one was 'the one'. If the break-up becomes acrimonious, Taurus can take this very badly, because it clashes with their basic need for harmony. Although capable of confrontation, even if they are the one to instigate a break-up, Taurus finds it hard to hurt the feelings of those they've once loved. Because of this they may not say much, which can make it difficult for their ex to understand why they're breaking up in the first place.

Taurus and . . .

♈ Aries

Taurus can benefit from a bit of Aries fire, and they both love the physical side of love, but arguments might arise from a clash in attitude towards money, so while an affair might work, a marriage could be tricky.

♋ Cancer

The ease of this combination rests in their both having a commitment to the security of home, creating a lasting bond. Equally sensual, this combination bodes well for a harmonious sex life, too.

♉ Taurus

The downside of this like-minded union might be boredom because even though both will be hard-working and affectionate, they might be missing the initial spark that gets things off the ground.

♌ Leo

Two big egos that are well matched in their physical appetites, this earth/fire combination can work well in the bedroom, but there may be some tension between Taurus' reticence and Leo's need for extravagant gestures.

♊ Gemini

Opposites attract and this earth/air combination could have wings, but probably only in the short-term, as Gemini's flighty attitude tends to clash badly with Taurus' more basic need for consistency and reliability.

♍ Virgo

There's a deep bond waiting to happen between these well-matched earth signs, with their equal love of continuity and order. Virgo may find Taurus a tad physical, but can gain from a more passionate awakening.

♉ Taurus

♎︎ Libra

Both signs are ruled by Venus and have a mutual love of beauty and the finer things in life. While there's an airiness to Libra that lifts Taurean earthiness, the attraction of this may be short lived, becoming an irritation over time.

♏︎ Scorpio

At first glance, there's not an obvious affiliation here but, in fact, both share a sexual bond that can make sparks fly. However, they are equally prone to streaks of possessiveness, which could cause friction.

♐︎ Sagittarius

There's never a dull moment between these two signs that are naturally attracted to each other sexually, but Sagittarius' freewheeling attitude may chafe against the usual Taurus desire for a quieter, home-based existence.

♑︎ Capricorn

Straightforward, physically complementary and sharing many similar goals, this combination may not be the most romantic but at its heart is an enduring friendship that is charmed by a well-matched sense of humour.

♒︎ Aquarius

The highly innovative, cerebral aspects of this unconventional and airy sign tend to clash with the more down-to-earth approach of Taurus, making this combination generally too restrictive for Aquarius to last much beyond a fling.

♓︎ Pisces

Both sensualists, there may be a tad too much watery imagination for earthy Taurus, but there will be an appreciation of Pisces' creative side, and this balance can also play out well in the bedroom.

Taurus love-o-meter

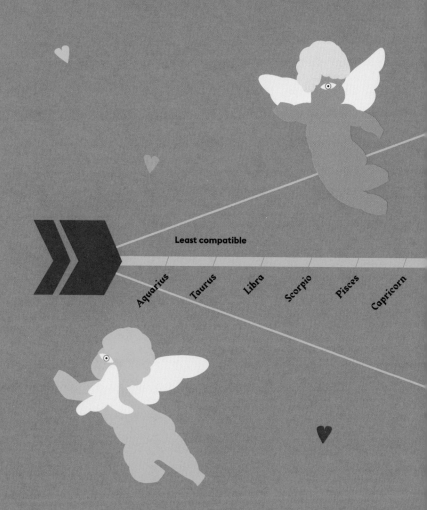

Least compatible

Aquarius Taurus Libra Scorpio Pisces Capricorn

Most compatible

Aries Sagittarius Gemini Leo Virgo Cancer

Gemini

*

The twins

21 MAY–20 JUNE

A mutable air sign symbolised by the twins, Gemini tends to see both sides of an argument, its speedy intellect influenced by its ruling planet Mercury. Tending to fight shy of commitment, this sign also epitomises a certain youthfulness of attitude.

OPPOSITE SIGN

Sagittarius

How does Gemini want to be loved?

Gemini wants to be loved for who they are, body, mind and soul, but they don't always realise that it's not easy for their lover to recognise which version of their many selves has come through the door. This keeps lovers on their toes, but it is also exhausting and it's a lot to ask of a companion, so Gemini needs to be aware of this and in order to get what they need, they may need to be prepared to meet their lover half way.

In their mind, Gemini has all the time in the world for languorous love-making, but the reality is that they can be so driven that love-making often gets relegated to the bottom of a list, somewhere after cleaning out the cat's litter tray and saving the world. Not very encouraging to a would-be lover, for sure, but knowing this about them means there's less likelihood of taking this predisposition quite so personally. Gemini's unpredictability about what they want and don't want can make them completely exasperating and this is a quandary for many when it comes to trying to love them. But any lover that can tactfully help Gemini take the pressure off themselves, creating some space just to be, will be welcomed with open arms. It's a fine balance to judge, however, and to complicate matters further this will probably only really be acceptable from a lover to whom Gemini has already made a commitment.

What kind of party will you find Gemini at?

The first to arrive, the last to leave, this airy, communicative sign is an astrological party animal. Large gatherings in which to mingle, chat and dance until sunrise appeal to Gemini's gregarious nature – as long as there are people, then the location, food and drink are pretty immaterial.

What is Gemini
like in bed?

Although not an overtly physical sign, Gemini loves to embrace and touch using their arms and hands and they also respond to hand, arm and shoulder massage, finding these body areas quite erotically charged. Curious, adventurous and spontaneous, they are naturally quite confident naked – sex can definitely be a light-hearted, exploratory affair for Gemini, and they are not averse to one-night stands. But while physical sex is there to be enjoyed, it is the meeting of minds that can spark sexual transcendence for Gemini. Erotic talk, too, may also feature in Gemini sex, as communicating in sound is particularly arousing and being read to can create a focus for foreplay.

The downside is that in spite of their spontaneity and openness to sex *en plein air* or on the kitchen floor, as the mood takes them, Gemini is often just too fast for the more painstaking and sensual lover who can find snacking on sex, rather than making it the main course, a bit disconcerting. Staying on schedule is all very well, but Gemini could do well to remember that there are some things that benefit from being savoured occasionally, and sex is one of them.

Moving in
with Gemini

If left to their own devices, Gemini is pretty easy going. Problems can arise, however, if those they are living with request some idea of what they are up to or where they are going. It's not that Gemini minds people knowing per se, it's just that they often haven't made up with own minds. This can make them appear rather secretive: because it's not important to them to make plans and stick to them, they can't really understand why it should matter to anyone else. However, while spontaneity and unpredictability are comfortable places for Gemini, they can be extremely disconcerting to others. It's sensible for Gemini to be mindful of this if they want to avoid alienating their partner.

Independent and outgoing, Gemini thrives on being social so are seldom holed up in their room for days on end and, as a result, their immediate domestic surroundings may be of only passing interest. An intermittent tendency to blitz through cleaning, however, may find their partner returning home to an unrecognisable space where their belongings have also been tidied up and reorganised to within an inch of their lives.

Breaking up
with Gemini

Gemini often feels that once they've made a decision that's it, so if they have decided their relationship is completely fine, they may become so busy with other things they misread the signs and a break-up can come as a complete surprise. Once confronted with the situation, their inclination is to rationalise and think their way through it, often refusing to consider their feelings (or anyone else's).

It's not that Gemini doesn't experience heartbreak, it's just that their strategy can be to rationalise their feelings to the point where they no longer feel them. If the boot is on the other foot, most Geminis don't vacillate but are swift executioners, even brutal, leaving no room for ambiguity. In this case, what is so obvious to them may come as a complete surprise to their partner. But in both cases the Gemini way is to throw it all up in the air and move on – fast.

Gemini and . . .

♈

Aries

Gemini's air gives oxygen to Aries' fire, and this is a free-spirited but hot-blooded combination that relies on friendship as much as lust. As long as Aries' decisiveness doesn't feel restrictive to Gemini, this can be a successful pairing.

♋

Cancer

Gemini's playfulness might prove too much for Cancer's need for security. Not knowing quite what's going on is the wind beneath Gemini's wings, but can be just too volatile for this sensitive sign, who prefers calmer waters.

♉

Taurus

Gemini can find the uncomplicated approach of this earth sign fascinating but not particularly compelling, and is likely to find the earthy Taurus a tad unchallenging for their more adventurous tastes.

♌

Leo

There's a good union to be enjoyed between these two outgoing, confident signs given to playful extroversion, both in and out of bed. But Leo's need to always be number one in Gemini's life may prove tricky to accommodate.

♊

Gemini

Twins meet twins, so they recognise each other, but this double dual combination might prove just too frenetic and flighty to last the course, especially when the relationship moves out of the bedroom.

♍

Virgo

Given they are both ruled by Mercury there's an initial mental affinity between them, but Gemini tends to find Virgo's detail-focused approach pernickety and boring, often making this a spiky combination from the word go.

♎ Libra

Intellectually, these two air signs create a lovely harmony. They are generally in agreement with each other and share a taste for travel and entertainment. Well matched sexually, there's a tolerance and ease that suits them both.

♏ Scorpio

There's immediate passion in the bedroom, but a problem outside it because Gemini's share-all nature conflicts with Scorpio's need for privacy. Unless this clash is managed with tact on both sides, it can herald the end before it starts.

♐ Sagittarius

They are each other's opposite sign, so the attraction is there and it's strong between their bodies and minds, but both are restless by nature and if this isn't recognised, it can inhibit any commitment between the two of them.

♑ Capricorn

The promise of order holds some attraction and this steadying influence can be good for Gemini, while Capricorn's sombre side can be lightened in return. It's a question of balance, though, and to reach that takes patience and tact.

♒ Aquarius

Because both share an airy, innovative approach to life and an inclination to unpredictability, this is an easy combination with an affection and appreciation for each other that can forge a happy and enduring bond.

♓ Pisces

There's lots of passion to be had here and it creates a potent attraction initially, but airy Gemini really doesn't understand Pisces' imagination and sensitivity and has a tendency to be irritated by their need for security.

Gemini

47

Gemini love-o-meter

Least compatible

Virgo Cancer Gemini Taurus Pisces Scorpio

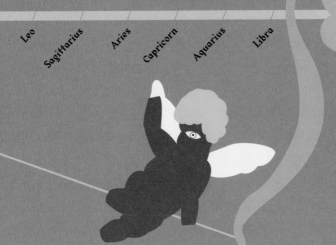

Most compatible

Leo · Sagittarius · Aries · Capricorn · Aquarius · Libra

Cancer

*

The crab

21 JUNE–21 JULY

Depicted by the crab and
the tenacity of its claws, Cancer is
a cardinal water sign, emotional
and intuitive, its sensitivity
protected by its shell. Ruled by
the maternal Moon, the shell also
represents the security of home,
to which Cancer is committed.

OPPOSITE SIGN

Capricorn

How does Cancer
want to be loved?

Often underestimated is the cautious side of Cancer, edging towards the water and then retreating is a typical characteristic when it comes to approaching love, so they have to be offered lots of reassurance – proof that it's worth the risk of getting wet. They never act before they're sure but when they are, that's it: committed. However tentative they are, though, once committed, Cancer will hold on tight and is loyal to a fault. Of course, then their expectation is to receive the same and they won't take kindly to being messed around. Never treat a Cancer mean to keep them keen; they don't like it and will be off. Game playing isn't particularly their style.

So, what is Cancer looking for? Sureness and kindness are key words; they need to know their partner cares. This highly sensual sign needs real passion, too, and you can't fake it, or Cancer will suss that out and any insincerity to boot. It's just that for any sort of transcendence in the bedroom there has to be a sense of security in the rest of the home, which is key for this creature ruled by the Moon and all its fluctuating influence. And romance is important, too, especially on first dates, where the moonlit mood weaves its own magic. Inevitably, one way to Cancer's heart is through their stomach, and the offer of a home-cooked meal can be even more welcome than one in a restaurant.

What kind of flowers should you buy Cancer?

White, sweet-scented jasmine, with its tenacity and capacity to embrace the walls of a home, and morning glory, are both Cancer flowers. Acanthus, too, with its pale white and mauve flowers, symbolises rebirth, immortality and healing.

What is Cancer like in bed?

In the bedroom, Cancer is a sensitive lover, happily focused on their partner's pleasure, empathetic and sometimes appearing almost too anxious to please, forgetting that sex is a two-way affair and that receiving creates as much pleasure as giving. This confident exterior is partly a defence, shielding a more sensitive, gentle soul. The more secure Cancer is, the more likely they are to relax and lose themselves in the moment; swept away from their immediate physical self on a tide of emotion.

Getting close to Cancer takes time, but it's always worth it. They like to take their time in the bedroom and it's seldom a quick event, more often a sensuous affair, and they are capable of being highly imaginative and playful once they're sure of their partner's commitment. Of course, casual sex can happen but primarily Cancer is all about the relationship in which sex can exist and flourish and communicate real feeling. Massage can be a key element of foreplay for Cancer, as attention to the physical body helps them open up and get past that protective, outer shell.

Moving in
with Cancer

Although domestically orientated, Cancer isn't necessarily the easiest sign to live with because their inner life is so active, it's not always obvious to partners what's going on inside that imaginative, intuitive mind. A quiet mood could mean happy introspection, thinking through a piece of work, or feeling upset. And while they find security in family and friends, Cancer needs quite a lot of downtime to process their feelings, sometimes to the exasperation of those around them who can easily misinterpret what's going on.

Cancer is also the proverbial collector, and this may show itself in a sentimental attachment to possessions that have no obvious meaning to anyone else but are important to them. So that collection of theatre programmes is essential, as is that chipped mug from childhood. Conversely, when the mood strikes, they can be abruptly, ruthlessly minimalist and have a massive clear out.

Breaking up
with Cancer

It can be very, very hard for Cancer to let go at the end of a relationship or love affair, irrespective of whether they are the one doing the breaking up. The problem with this rather indecisive style is that it can send out mixed messages and cause more hurt to both parties in the long run. And in a reaction to all this emotion, the crab can retreat and scuttle off, completely disappearing emotionally in order to try and cope.

They may also do this if they are the one who is dumped, refusing any love and support from well-meaning family or friends, shutting them out while they hurt inside. It's very much all or nothing with Cancer, it's the way they cope, but emotions need to be expressed and they will, in the end, do so and move on.

Cancer and . . .

♈ Aries

The sexual attraction between this fire and water sign combination can be steamy, but Aries may find Cancer's tendency towards defensiveness inhibiting, while the crab's liking for domesticity can fuel Aries' desire for escape.

♉ Taurus

Both find the affection they seek in each other and are sexually well suited. Cancer can bring out a more imaginative side to steady Taurus and, in return, Cancer's tendency towards moodiness is well grounded and tolerated.

♊ Gemini

Although initially attracted to Gemini, they can be just too fickle for the security-seeking crab. Their intellect tends to clash with Cancer's intuitive take on life, although that intriguing airiness can ventilate some of their thinking.

♋ Cancer

They understand each other but, with so much in common, how will it pan out? In bed, they're a sensual match, but elsewhere there may just be too much possessiveness and need, unless they're able to take a step back occasionally.

♌ Leo

There's a wonderful optimism to Leo that attracts Cancer, but in the long run that continual exuberance and need for public adulation can be troublesome to a soul prone to sensitivity and with a need for reassurance.

♍ Virgo

Because Virgo's attention to detail chimes with Cancer's need for security, and the balance between emotion and intellect are there, this is a harmonious and affectionate bond from the start.

Libra

When Cancer's emotional take on love meets Libra's intellectual need for balance this can cause friction, and understanding each other's needs can be tricky. A commitment to creating a beautiful home helps, but it may not be enough.

Capricorn

Astrological opposites always tend to attract, at least initially, but Capricorn's reserve and self-reliance can be interpreted as rejection by Cancer, which makes for an uneasy alliance over time.

Scorpio

These two signs understand each other, and Cancer's commitment and affection make Scorpio feel very secure, reducing the potential sting in their tail and allowing for the physical and emotional intimacy they both thrive on.

Aquarius

Way too prone to be detached, intellectual and unpredictable to meet Cancer's basic need for attention, Aquarius may be of interest sexually but isn't often emotionally engaged enough to allow this to endure much past the bedroom.

Sagittarius

Cancer tends to find this fire sign's flighty nature makes them feel too insecure, while their more sensitive, domestic side tends to grate on freedom-loving Sagittarius' nerves. In the long term, they make better friends than lovers.

Pisces

Both imaginative water signs but in different ways – one a doer and the other a worker – they are also sensually compatible, Cancer's protectiveness happily supporting Pisces' romantic vision. They understand and work well together.

Cancer love-o-meter

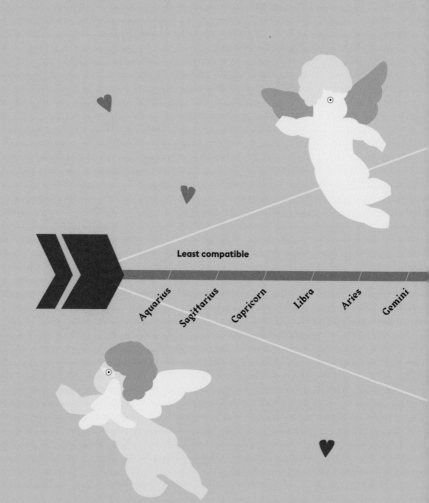

Least compatible

Aquarius

Sagittarius

Capricorn

Libra

Aries

Gemini

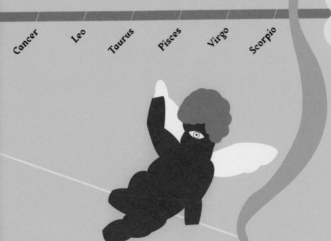

Most compatible

Cancer   Leo   Taurus   Pisces   Virgo   Scorpio

Leo

✳

The lion

22 JULY–21 AUGUST

A fixed fire sign, ruled by the Sun, Leo loves to shine and is an idealist at heart, positive and generous to a fault. Depicted by the lion, Leo can roar with pride and be confident and uncompromising, with a great faith and trust in humanity.

OPPOSITE SIGN

Aquarius

How does Leo want to be loved?

Put simply, adoringly and unconditionally. At first glance, this looks very simple but Leo is more complicated than they look and also one of the proudest signs of the zodiac, which can make them vulnerable. In fact, Leo's apparent need for unconditional adoration, and their reaction when they don't get it, can come from a deep insecurity, in spite of all the outgoing brashness.

Because of this paradox, loving Leo can be a bit of a challenge, and it can take a lot longer than it might first appear to get them to commit. If Leo has a bit of a reputation as being commitment-phobic, this can sometimes come from an inability to fully trust that they are lovable. And because they seem so self-confident, this aspect of the lion sometimes gets covered up in a don't-care attitude. Sometimes it takes a bit of grounded patience to get through these self-imposed barriers.

Leo is also about having fun, fun, fun; so this welcomes handling with a light touch. Not given to huge introspection like some of the watery signs, Leo will respond well to dates that involve straightforward activities: whether it's a luxury dinner, funny movie, playing Twister or charades – Leo has a child-like appreciation for fun. Doing things together and creating relationships based on mutually shared interests and activities – like a love of rock climbing or salsa dancing – can be a great way of loving Leo. Given all this, Leo partners aren't for the faint hearted, but behind that ego is a loving, caring, loyal lover – remember, many lions mate for life so they sometimes take their time playing the field first.

What kind of pet should you get with Leo?

Any feline. From the pedigree Persian and the supercilious Siamese to the domestic tabby and ginger moggy, it's got to be a cat with Leo. This pet has exactly the right amount of independence and playfulness, and the old adage 'a cat may look at a king' sums up the relationship between a cat and its Leo owner.

What is Leo
like in bed?

For a sensuous sign like Leo, sex is a pleasure to make them purr and sometimes roar and no better place to start than with their back. For Leo, in particular, this is an erogenous area, and massaging the full length of the spine to the buttocks is a wonderful start. There's definitely a sense of performance but there's also a generosity because Leo likes to give as much as to receive in the bedroom: it's all part of their regal beneficence. A part of Leo's sensuality is to look, so a full black-out is unlikely – and they also enjoy hearing how good it all is, not only when talking dirty but also in praise afterwards. All in all, making love is a very inclusive business for Leo, and their focus is definitely on sharing a great experience.

Leo may be sexy but they also understand the importance of romance. So the lighting may be in candle form, and the foreplay is seldom skimped. This is also an adventurous sign that isn't above a little risk taking, so *en plein air* sex may be on the cards, or sex in unexpected places. It's often fun too, for Leo, who is quite capable of laughing their partners into bed before anyone realises quite how serious it's getting.

Moving in
with Leo

Never a dull moment, living with Leo, except when they're asleep.
In theory, once you get the hang of them, this good-natured sign
is easy to be around, as not much seems to bother them. But it might
bother partners when they endlessly leave towels on the bathroom
floor or the washing up stacked next to the sink as they rush out
on yet another big adventure ... or perhaps just because they are
late for work.

Rotas for chores don't really work for Leo, because the
king of the jungle probably has other things on their mind and
such domestic minutiae can be of little consequence. However,
the contradiction is that Leo actually wants to live in lovely
surroundings so isn't by nature slovenly, it's just that they would
prefer someone else to do the domestic donkey-work as, frankly,
they probably think it's a little beneath them. If one of you suggests
hiring a cleaner, you can bet it's going to be Leo. If there are any
difficulties between you, Leo will let you know, but they seldom
hold a grudge; their roar is much worse than their bite and
quarrels are quickly forgotten.

♌

Leo

Breaking up
with Leo

There's no way a break-up will be without drama, but a lion in pain tends to roar, whether they've got a splinter in their paw or a life-threatening wound. Another Leo reaction to a break-up is to ignore it: pretend they're absolutely fine and didn't care anyway, even though inside that heart can be badly wounded. Whether they're roaring or quietly seething, they often try to show the world they don't care by throwing themselves into extravagant, exhausting socialising. The good thing about Leo is that their bruised heart recovers quickly, and it won't be long before they're back dating. In their magnanimous way, Leo tends to expect to be friends with their exes further down the line.

Leo

Leo and . . .

♈

Aries

These two fire signs are often considered a match made in heaven, apart from one thing: their equally large egos. However, if they can use their natural rapport to overcome this in the bedroom and elsewhere, it's a very happy union.

♋

Cancer

Romance dominates this relationship and it can be harmonious with Leo's need for adoration well met by Cancer's loyalty and intensity. But Leo needs to be mindful that a desire for public acknowledgement makes Cancer insecure.

♉

Taurus

This coupling can be troubled by an immediate clash between Leo's flamboyance and Taurus' natural caution, after which the bull's stubbornness in their attempt to bring the lion down to earth may end in tears for both. Too tricky for many.

♌

Leo

If they can overcome the natural inclination toward rivalry that comes from two big egos, this can be a very exciting and intense affair, but they need to work out who is in charge, or take it in turns, otherwise the passion could burn itself out.

♊

Gemini

Independence, joie de vivre and glamour mark this pairing with a sense of fun, which may be difficult to transfer from the bedroom to the real world. But if airy Gemini can make a commitment to Leo's demanding ways, it can work well.

♍

Virgo

An unlikely fit, because the cool intelligence of Virgo and refusal to get excited about speculative plans can dampen Leo's exuberant nature, while Virgo's finesse and attention to detail bewilders Leo, who is all about the big picture.

♎︎ Libra

Both share a love of beautiful things and that aesthetic appreciation gives them a lot in common. Plus, Leo's dominance doesn't irritate Libra, who rather likes someone else to make the decisions, both in and out of the bedroom.

♑︎ Capricorn

It's not an easy union between Leo's glamorous take on life and Capricorn's rather practical approach, making the latter seem rather disapproving to the former. And given their basic positions, there's little compromise either.

♏︎ Scorpio

There can be a bit of a stand-off here, between Leo's carefree, outgoing attitude and Scorpio's inclination to be rather intense and secretive. That clash in basic temperament isn't easy for either one to understand, or to placate.

♒︎ Aquarius

Despite an initial attraction that may get them into bed, Leo needs a lover who at least feigns devotion. Aquarius' airy indifference leaves them feeling bemused and, in the end, rejected. Leo just needs to be needed and Aquarius doesn't.

Leo

♐︎ Sagittarius

Similarly given to freedom and adventure, these two recognise an optimism and expansiveness in each that unites and excites them, including in the bedroom, where their fiery natures keep the passion going long after first meeting.

♓︎ Pisces

Leo struggles with Pisces' mystical side which is so completely at odds with their need to be socialising on a public stage. Without a compromise, Leo's extroversion tends to clash with Pisces' need for a more contemplative life.

Leo love-o-meter

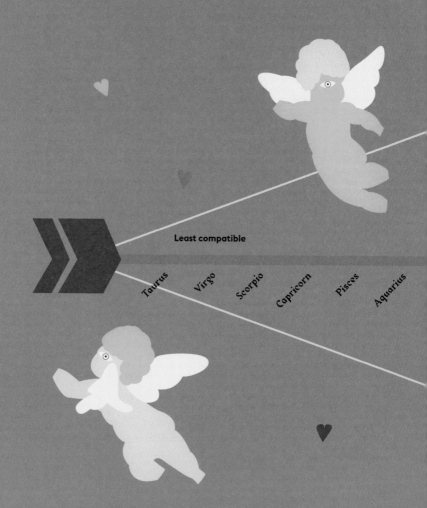

Least compatible

Taurus Virgo Scorpio Capricorn Pisces Aquarius

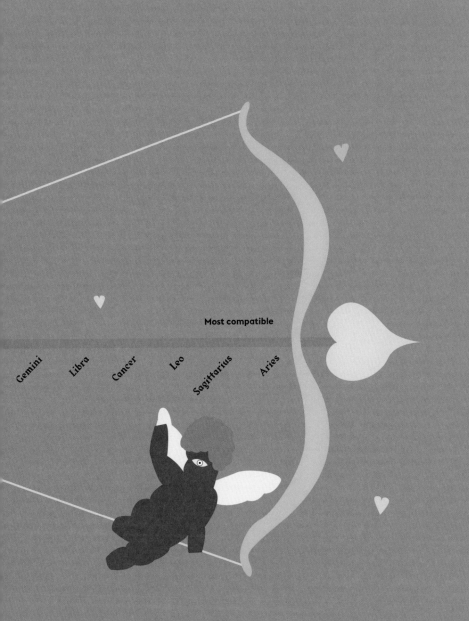

Most compatible

Gemini Libra Cancer Leo Sagittarius Aries

Virgo

*

The virgin

22 AUGUST–21 SEPTEMBER

Traditionally represented as
a maiden or virgin, this mutable
earth sign is observant, detail
oriented and tends towards self-
sufficiency. Ruled by Mercury, Virgo
benefits from a sharp intellect that
can be self-critical, while often
being very health conscious.

OPPOSITE SIGN

Pisces

How does Virgo want to be loved?

The self-restraint typical of many Virgos can make it difficult for them to ask for the love and affection they need, but they are capable of very deep, grounded relationships. Consequently, Virgo can feel hurt when their gentle reserve or practical attitude to love gets misinterpreted as a dismissal, although they're unlikely to show it. It's only when Virgo feels truly loved that they feel secure enough to let go of their defensive behaviour and become less inhibited and more passionate. It's not always easy, though: many a would-be lover has feared getting it wrong or being criticised by Virgo, making it difficult to make the first move. Virgo actually hates to hurt other people's feelings and doesn't always realise they are doing so, purely because they are so damned logical.

Getting past this first hurdle takes patience on behalf of any would-be lover. Virgo also has to consider all the evidence that might mean this person *isn't* Mr or Miss Right. Because of this, they can have a tendency to be very discriminating, if not picky, with a checklist of requirements that can look superficial to others – but is just due diligence to Virgo! Wear the wrong socks and you may not merit consideration, regardless of the fact that they adore you.

When this Virgo inclination for thinking things through turns into overthinking, they can be their own worst enemy. It's then that their hyper-logical approach can get in the way of the need for Virgo to occasionally compromise to get what they want – which is to be loved completely and passionately by someone who sees beyond their self-imposed restrictions.

What colour should you wear on a date with Virgo?

Blue or orange, either colour blocked, or subtly used in a classic pin-stripe detail, for example. Wear these colours to attract Virgo energy, choosing accessories – shoes, gloves, socks, hat or even underwear – if you don't have other clothes in these colours.

What is Virgo like in bed?

As you'd expect from a sign that enjoys planning events, lovers can feel very cherished by Virgo's attention to detail. Yes, Virgo can do spontaneous and uninhibited because they are also an adaptable sign, but they do like to stage-manage things a bit because, when pleasure's at stake, it's worth taking a little trouble, surely? But there's a big difference between taking a little trouble and giving stage directions in bed and sometimes Virgo just has to do the diplomatic thing and keep quiet.

The instinct to give 100 per cent to their partner makes Virgo a sensitive lover, as long as they can resist mentally checking all is going well and just abandon themselves to the moment. Virgo also needs to remember that receiving pleasure is as important as giving when it comes to making love, and the bedroom is one place where perfection really doesn't matter because it's all about trust and sharing and creating something special between the two people in the room and them alone. But the more secure Virgo feels in a relationship, the more easily they relax in the bedroom, and that's when the erotic magic can really happen.

Moving in with Virgo

That practicality and thoughtfulness they're famous for should make Virgo a dream housemate, right? Think again, because in some cases, that organisational side of Virgo isn't always evident in their living environment. Their minds might be tidy, they might always show up neatly dressed, the bathtub might be pristine and there's no mouldy food in the fridge, but their room may be as chaotic as the proverbial teenager's. While order is important in some areas, sentimentality can win the day in others, and throwing things out isn't always the Virgo way, which can lead to a lot of personal clutter.

Where they live and who they live with is definitely important to Virgo, but they may not be very expressive about this. That reserved nature means they don't always say how much their partner means to them, but they'll be first to show their commitment in deeds. They'll also be up for late-night discussions on both national politics or the latest TV celebrity gossip, analysing the human behaviour of both, and will happily hear you out on your problems at work through to the wee small hours.

Breaking up
with Virgo

Virgo is not a clingy sign and can tend to appear rather stoic about break-ups. Despite this, they are often stunned when they have to experience a relationship falling apart, because, like everything else in life, they believe they should have been able to fix it. They also have a tendency to rationalise and bury their feelings to protect themselves, so it's not always obvious how hurt they are. If they've instigated the break up, Virgo will not do so without very good reason – but this may be more obvious to them than to their ex. Under pressure, the Virgo instinct is to control the situation – whichever side is doing the breaking up – which can actually make things worse. Better to gracefully let things go.

Virgo

Virgo and . . .

♈

Aries

There's an immediate tension here between prudent Virgo and impulsive Aries that can create an emotional uneasiness between them, even when there's a strong intellectual connection and attraction.

♉

Taurus

Between these two earth signs lies a nice harmony as both have a practical inclination but also a sensual streak. Creating a secure future together means creating a lovely home, on which they both agree and can easily live happily ever after.

♊

Gemini

Their intellectual approach to life means there's an immediate affinity, but Virgo tends to find Gemini's airiness unpredictable, while Virgo's earthy nature is a bit too stuck in the mud. Without a lot of thought, this relationship can be tricky.

♋

Cancer

This is a happy, loving combination, as both recognise each other's hidden sensuality, and make a good match in their need for domestic harmony. Virgo's protective streak suits affectionate Cancer, who also makes Virgo feel secure.

♌

Leo

Leo's exuberance can be too much for Virgo's reserved nature, both in the bedroom and the domestic purse. Guarding against extravagance irritates Leo and temperamentally they are ill-suited unless they proceed with care.

♍

Virgo

With so much in common, it can be a relief for Virgo to fall in love with Virgo and they will talk as much as anything else in the bedroom. They are so well and happily matched that the only fly in the ointment may be a jostling for first place.

♎ Libra

Virgo's natural reserve is tricky for Libra to understand and they can interpret this as a rebuff, even when it's not the case, while Virgo feels that Libra's love of the good things in life is too frivolous. This combination needs careful handling.

♑ Capricorn

There's an immediate harmony between the happy diligence of these two earth signs. They like and respect each other's purposeful approach to life and love, and intuitively they recognise a need for approval and mutual achievement.

♏ Scorpio

Even while they admire each other's minds, the highly logical nature of Virgo makes it difficult to accept Scorpio's more imaginative ways, although there is a deep appreciation for their loyalty, which can help override any conflict.

♒ Aquarius

Although of similar intellectual approach, each can be rather remote and together this gets exaggerated. Virgo's practical ambitions are not well matched by Aquarius' more cerebral engagement with life, which can create problems.

♐ Sagittarius

The reckless traveller is difficult for hard-working Virgo to understand, and troubling to their need to put down roots. Even with a closely aligned intellect, clashes are likely to be deep-seated, considering their different temperaments.

♓ Pisces

There may be too many opposites to overcome between these two, as Virgo's more precise ways tend to clash with Pisces all-encompassing view of life's possibilities, while their dreaminess can irritate Virgo's practicality.

 Virgo

Virgo love-o-meter

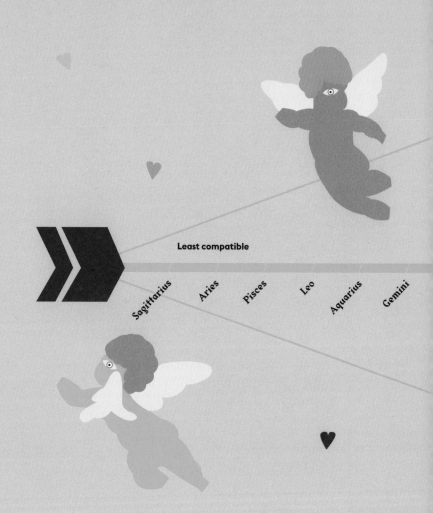

Least compatible

Sagittarius   Aries   Pisces   Leo   Aquarius   Gemini

Most compatible

Libra　　*Scorpio*　　*Capricorn*　　*Cancer*　　*Taurus*　　*Virgo*

Libra

*

The scales

22 SEPTEMBER–21 OCTOBER

A cardinal air sign, ruled by Venus,
Libra is all about beauty, balance
(as depicted by the scales) and
harmony in its rather romanticised,
ideal world. With a strong aesthetic
sense, Libra can be both arty and
crafty, but also likes fairness
and can be very diplomatic.

OPPOSITE SIGN

Aries

How does Libra want to be loved?

Ruled by Venus, the goddess of love, Libra is all about the romance of love. They love romancing and being romanced, and they feel much more balanced generally when they are in love or in a loving relationship, and a little out of sorts when not. This can sometimes mean that Libra likes to be in love for love's sake, delighting in the romance while sometimes losing sight of the relationship itself (or its more tedious aspects, like putting the rubbish out).

Libra is a sign that loves to be admired, and even worshipped, as much from a distance as close up, partly because in spite of all their apparent social ease, they are not always the most self-confident of signs. Constant reassurance suggests they're needy, but it's not so much that, it's just that the endless internal weighing up of the situation can undermine their self-worth. Even while Libra tends to have good instincts generally, they are sometimes afraid to trust them. Talking about the relationship with their partner is sometimes done in an effort to make it all seem more real, grounded and trustworthy.

As something of an idealist, Libra also tends to project their ideals onto their partner, which can make it easy for them to be disappointed; and to keep the reality of their relationship at arm's length. Deep down however, they are as vulnerable as any to the pursuit of real love. Don't be fooled by that Libra charm and gloss; their reserve creates a bit of a 'look but don't touch' coolness, but when they find someone who will allow them to let their guard down, this sign makes a great lover.

Where should you take Libra on a mini-break?

To relax, Libra needs beautiful surroundings and intellectual stimulation, making a cultural tour, with lots of art, architecture or music, a serious contender, especially when it comes to city breaks. Music festivals can appeal too but there will need to be some serious glamping on offer, as Libra and muddy fields are seldom a good mix!

What is Libra
like in bed?

Sex for Libra is seldom focused just on the body but also needs
a strong mental connection, so much so that even talking about sex
can be very arousing. Erotic pleasure is often quite creative, with
Libra paying a lot of attention to seduction and foreplay. The skin
is very sensitive and being stroked and massaged can easily turn
Libra on, especially the back, the lower back and the buttocks, all
of which are markedly erogenous areas of their body. As much as
being pleased, Libra gains a great deal of pleasure from pleasing
their partner, and watching their partner's sexual pleasure. Mutual
enjoyment definitely makes lovemaking more erotic for Libra,
which in turn makes them unselfish lovers.

Libra needs to feel they're appreciated, though, and they need
to hear encouraging words, to which they happily respond. Libra
can often be quite reserved and discriminating, in spite of appearing
so sexually confident and up front about what they want. They
need a balance, but there's a subtle line and anything too crude
or aggressive can sometimes be a turn off. Romance and verbal
exchange fire up sexual attraction for Libra, while compliments
and flattery in the bedroom helps fuel this further.

Moving in with Libra

Living with Libra is, in theory, pretty easy, but the demand for a harmonious life can sometimes be very much on their terms. This trait may not be immediately obvious, because they can be so charming and are willing to discuss and debate issues, but often housemates find themselves persuaded into agreeing just to end the conversation!

Home isn't as much of a priority as it is to some of the other signs, but how it looks matters deeply to Libra and even if they don't have a sentimental attachment to things, they will still want the best that they can afford. Their personal taste may make them quite fussy about where housemates leave their things, and cluttering up beautifully arranged objets d'art won't go down well with Libra, who can find sharing space tricky because of this.

Generally well disposed to being clean and tidy, Libra will go a long way to avoid an argument about whose turn it is to do the washing up or hoover the stairs, sometimes just by doing it themselves. In spite of a tendency to shy away from conflict, if they feel they are being treated unfairly, then Libra hackles can rise and squabbles can occur – but it does take quite a lot to provoke outright confrontation.

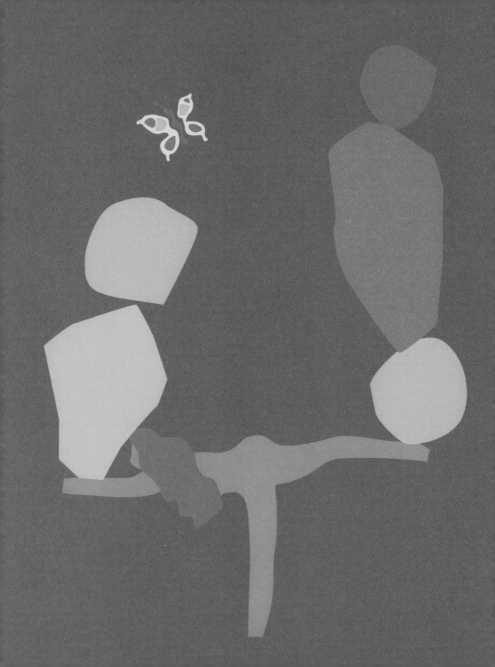

Breaking up
with Libra

Libra is the sign of partnerships and can be very invested in a relationship for its own sake. They may hang on until it is well past its sell-by date because they are often as committed to the relationship itself as they are to the person concerned. They also hate to hurt anyone's feelings. While break-ups are tough for everyone, Libra always wants to try to understand why it has happened, and the reasons for it. Like other air signs that try to think their way through a problem, Libra often tries to work out how they, or their partner, are feeling, but it's just not always possible. This can be a hard lesson for Libra, but something that can actually be learnt from a break-up, irrespective of who wants to break up from whom.

Libra

Libra and . . .

♈

Aries

The physical connection between air and fire can easily ignite, but although for Libra there's often an initial attraction to Aries' passion, there can occasionally be friction between them because of Libra's more reserved style.

♉

Taurus

There's a real connection here in a mutual love of art and music, and, both being ruled by Venus, there's an appreciation of life's luxuries. And although there's a good sexual connection too, Libra can sometimes find Taurus' earthy approach a little heavy.

♊

Gemini

There's a lightness in this happy combination, as both air signs take pleasure in flirting and while there's probably a lot more talk than action, thanks to their mutual inclination toward indecision, they will eventually charm each other into bed.

♋

Cancer

Cancer's watery need for emotional responsiveness may be a challenge for airy Libra, whose commitment to the home tends to be fairly superficial compared to the crab's, requiring thoughtfulness on both sides to avoid misunderstanding.

♌

Leo

Libra is tactful enough to manage Leo's hot-blooded ego, and their mutual playfulness and love of socialising creates an instantaneous initial bond on which to build. However, that inner reserve is no match for the lion's sensual fire.

♍

Virgo

There can be too much light-heartedness in Libra's airy approach for the rather serious, earthy Virgo. Although the initial attraction of opposites can work well, it just needs some give and take on both sides to get beyond their basic differences.

Libra

While they easily recognise each other, there's not much to ground them, so it can feel as if they are playing at love, rather than really feeling it. When it comes to balance, they may need more from their partner to get beyond that first attraction.

Capricorn

Initially tricky, there can be an immediate clash because Capricorn isn't always able to see beyond Libra's more frivolous exterior, but this can sometimes be overcome by a strong physical connection, thanks to the realistic nature of the goat.

Scorpio

Love between these two can be pretty heady at first, but that sting in the tail might be too much for diplomatic Libra, and their rather airy, flirtatious approach to sex might not find a balance in sensual Scorpio's intense attitude.

Aquarius

These two air signs have much in common but it's the experimental side of Aquarius that initially piques Libra's interest, waking them up to new ideas and experiences. Harmonious friendship underpins any relationship here.

Sagittarius

Romance features strongly when these two pair up, with Sagittarius finding Libra's intellect and charm intriguing and difficult to resist. In turn, the fire sign's outgoing and adventurous attitude appeals, freeing up Libra's reserve.

Pisces

A strong romantic connection gets them off to a good start, but Pisces' sentimental side can sometimes irritate outgoing Libra who needs to socialise, and isn't always able to reassure Pisces that they really care enough as they head for the door.

Libra love-o-meter

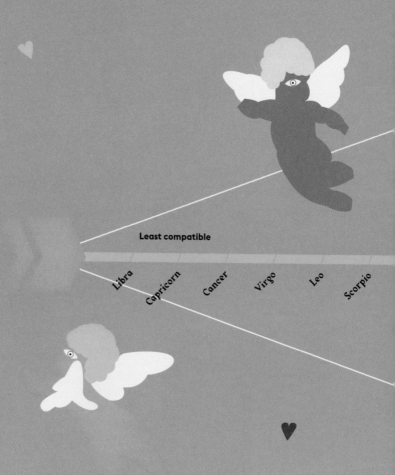

Least compatible

Libra   Capricorn   Cancer   Virgo   Leo   Scorpio

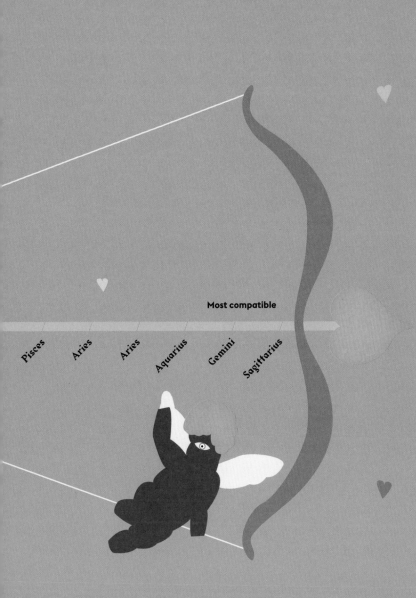

Most compatible

Pisces Aries Aries Aquarius Gemini Sagittarius

Scorpio

*

The scorpion

22 OCTOBER–21 NOVEMBER

Given to intense feelings, as befits
a fixed water sign, Scorpio is
depicted by the scorpion – linking
it to the rebirth that follows death –
and is ruled by both Pluto and Mars.
With a strong spirituality and deep
emotions, Scorpio needs security
to transform its strength.

OPPOSITE SIGN

Taurus

How does Scorpio want to be loved?

Scorpio wants to be loved completely, passionately, emotionally and physically – that's all! If that sounds like a tall order, then it's because they are given to being the most intense sign of the zodiac, prepared to invest everything in a relationship that they hope will sustain them on every level.

None of this is necessarily obvious, thanks to Scorpio's secretive side. Ruled by Pluto, the god of the underworld, Scorpio may struggle to convey how they want to be loved, and this may make them feel very vulnerable and sometimes unnecessarily defensive. The focus of their desire may have no idea how Scorpio feels, until they choose to strike. And, once they've declared themselves, Scorpio would like immediate reciprocation on which to base their trust. This can be tricky as it can take others, especially those who are more cautious about love, a while to catch up and feel as equally in love as Scorpio. For sanity's sake, Scorpio must remember this, otherwise they are likely to assume a rejection when none exists, just because their partner doesn't show immediate commitment.

Loving Scorpio can be intensely rewarding but their constant need for reassurance can be difficult to understand. Trust takes a while to establish for Scorpio and it can sometimes feel to their partner as if their commitment is being constantly challenged. It may be. Fortunately, once Scorpio does feel loved and feels that their devotion, affection and loyalty are reciprocated, they can relax.

What day of the week should you call Scorpio?

Tuesday – the day named after Mars, the god of war, which we see more obviously in the French word for Tuesday, Mardi. Although ruled by Pluto, Scorpio is also associated with the strong planet Mars, which is why Tuesday is their lucky day.

What is Scorpio like in bed?

There's a real chamber of secrets to be explored with Scorpio, but it's also important to remember that sex isn't just about the physical side of love for them, or not very often. Usually there's a strong spiritual undertow to sex for Scorpio, and its transformative power to change or secure a relationship means that a one-night stand is of little interest. Sex for them usually has to be within the terms of a relationship towards which they (if not their partner) have already made a commitment.

Once in bed, however, there can be an intensity and passion seldom matched by other signs, but also a playful curiosity and willingness to listen and explore a partner's needs as much as their own, making them great in bed. However, this isn't the sign of straightforward foreplay, it's always a bit of a mysterious dance, which may need to be played out long before getting to sex. In fact, because of their secretive side, Scorpio may appear to give more than they receive in bed, at least initially, but it's also their way of encouraging their partner's commitment. Long intense looks, lots of kissing and caressing, Scorpio likes to savour every sensual moment.

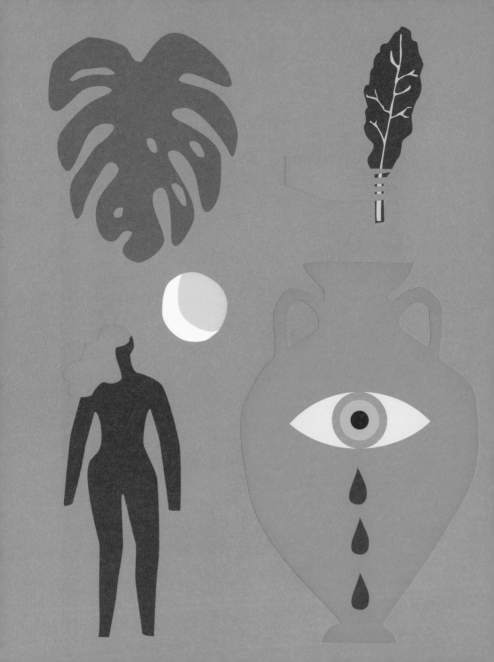

Moving in
with Scorpio

Scorpio often overlooks their partner's domestic quirks because they are curious about and ready to consider the reasons behind other people's behaviours. This can make them open-minded and easy to live with, unless this trait is exploited. Abuse it and that sting could be lethal!

It's also true that while Scorpio doesn't suffer fools gladly, they often keep their own counsel and will just disappear from a situation they don't like. This can give Scorpio the reputation for being moody, but if they don't want to continue a discussion or participate socially, they won't. This isn't sulking, just a need to replenish their inner energy, which can get sapped by too many demands. Time out and time alone is often the way Scorpio will recuperate, and this need shouldn't be taken personally.

This complex mix of needing lots of intense one-to-one communication, coupled with a need for privacy, can be perplexing. Scorpio needs to remember that how they're feeling isn't always obvious to their partner, who may misjudge the situation as a consequence.

Breaking up
with Scorpio

The downside of the need for a deep connection to another person, and Scorpio's tendency toward possessiveness, can make a break-up very difficult indeed. Trust is always an issue for Scorpio. It may not look like it, but a lot of work has gone on before they trust someone, so if this is betrayed it's always hard. Scorpio is also a fixed sign, so adjusting to any change is tricky, and something has to be really dead before they will let go. There is often a series of attempts to bring a relationship back to life before finally letting it go, and this can prolong the agony.

♏

Scorpio

Scorpio and . . .

♈

Aries

Sexual sparks fly between these two, but despite this initial attraction, Scorpio's more emotional, secretive side tends to exasperate open-hearted and free-spirited Aries, who can seem a little superficial to the deeper-minded water sign.

♋

Cancer

Scorpio's need for affection and devotion is well matched by Cancer's need for security, and while the crab can be rather passive, it responds well to Scorpio's possessiveness and passionate ardour, making this a well-matched combination.

♉

Taurus

There's a shared trait of stubbornness and jealousy here that could cause problems, which would be a shame because Scorpio relishes Taurus' earthy desire and sexual stamina, and Taurus enjoys the deeper emotional connection.

♌

Leo

The physical attraction is very strong, but Leo's extravagance and need for romantic gestures is at odds with Scorpio's need for a deeper erotic connection, which creates a potential clash that could be difficult to overcome between these two driven types.

♊

Gemini

There's an element of flightiness to Gemini that can undermine Scorpio's need for total commitment, and this challenge to their emotional security might outweigh the initial attraction Scorpio has to a more social butterfly.

♍

Virgo

Deep feelings and a natural inclination toward commitment in both these signs create a bond on which a good relationship can be built, as long as Virgo doesn't try to restrict the more intellectual or sensual aspects of Scorpio's personality.

Libra

This can be a tricky pairing because while Libra is often interested by Scorpio's intellectual and sexual intensity, Scorpio's need for commitment isn't easily met by Libra, who finds Scorpio's inclination to be jealous and too demanding.

Capricorn

Both are equally serious about being on the same emotional team, with an almost equal need for security, while Scorpio's passionate intensity balances Capricorn's more brooding approach to sex, making this a compatible pairing.

Scorpio

Unless they recognise that it is their similarities that create difficulties from the word go, this pairing will eventually sting their relationship to death with a mismatch of moods, secrets and possessiveness, in spite of their sexual compatibility.

Aquarius

Scorpio's deep, emotional demands conflict with Aquarius' open-hearted approach to love (and sex), and Scorpio finds this intellectual airiness undermining, tending to make them feel too insecure to tolerate anything more than a brief affair.

Sagittarius

At first, Sagittarius' freewheeling, fun-loving attitude is deeply attractive to Scorpio, but it will rankle in time if Scorpio's need for security isn't met because of Sagittarius' constant pursuit of travel and new adventures in body and mind.

Pisces

There's a nice balance here between Scorpio's strong, silent aspect and Pisces' rather indecisive take on life, while their sexual attraction is imaginative and romantic and their tendency to feel emotions deeply makes them both feel secure.

Scorpio love-o-meter

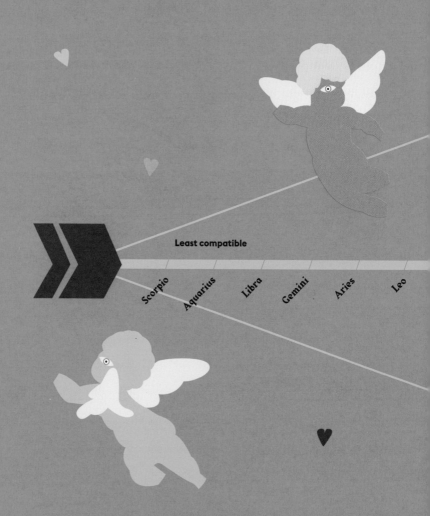

Least compatible

Scorpio Aquarius Libra Gemini Aries Leo

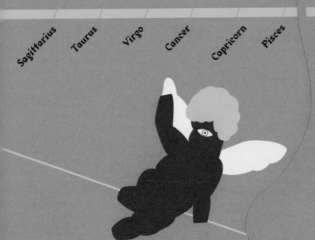

Most compatible

Sagittarius Taurus Virgo Cancer Capricorn Pisces

Sagittarius

✳

The archer

22 NOVEMBER–21 DECEMBER

Depicted by the archer, Sagittarius
is a mutable fire sign that's all about
travel and adventure, in body or
mind, and is very direct in approach.
Ruled by the benevolent Jupiter,
Sagittarius is optimistic with lots
of ideas; liking a free rein, but
with a tendency to generalise.

OPPOSITE SIGN

Gemini

How does Sagittarius want to be loved?

Open-hearted almost to a fault, with a huge capacity for adventure (and an occasional tendency to bolt), Sagittarius appears to think that everyone else is just like them. Consequently, they tend to send mixed messages and it can take a while to work out how they want to be loved. Sagittarius also expects love to be somewhat elusive, something in the distance found after an adventure or journey along an unexplored path. They expect to chase and be chased – after all, that's half the fun of love, isn't it? But while the chase is pretty important, it's a chase that leads to a conclusion, right? That's the problematic bit: Sagittarius isn't always so sure.

Sagittarius wants to be loved for their mind as much as anything else. They really value having someone to share and discuss things with. In fact, being loved as a friend can be the first step to getting close to Sagittarius, although if this is anything other than genuine, they'll know.

Just like everyone else, however, Sagittarius needs to feel loved and secure about it, even if they don't always show it. And, in fact, their independent streak may sometimes be something of an unconscious defence against being disappointed or hurt. It's not that they want to be tamed, they don't, but a secure place to lay their head actually appeals as much as wide-open spaces. These apparent contradictions are easier to understand if you think of the psychological metaphor of their personality, the horse. Loving Sagittarius can be deeply rewarding if you share their yearning for travel and adventure, whether in body or mind.

What kind of party will you find Sagittarius at?

You might have to travel to party with the archer, as Sagittarius will be the first to take a flight just for a 24-hour rave before taking the red-eye back to the office. If you do catch them, when it comes to buying them a cocktail with an equine kick, try something with ginger at its heart, like a bourbon-based Old Fashioned.

What is Sagittarius like in bed?

There's a playfulness about Sagittarius' approach to life that extends into the bedroom. Sex is another form of communication, as far as they're concerned, and like any good conversation it can vary – short and to the point, long and languid, flirty, exploratory, intense, fun – but seldom taken too seriously. Sagittarius very often sees sex in such a straightforward way, they can rather miss the point of its emotional connection as they are already thinking about the next big idea, plan or adventure. All of which can give this sign something of a reputation for fickleness.

Sagittarius has a lot of sexual energy, but at heart is quite relaxed. They're not going to fuss too much unless it's a big romantic event like an engagement or anniversary – there's always going to be another time, either with the one they're with, or with someone else. What's for sure is that they are so cheerful, thoughtful and easy to be with, that as long as they don't get asked for more than they can offer emotionally, Sagittarius generally makes a great lover.

Moving in
with Sagittarius

On one level, Sagittarius is easy and actually loves to live communally. But they also often choose to spend quite a lot of time away from home, travelling for work, for example.

This is all well and good unless partners want a little more commitment, whether that is Sagittarius doing their share of the communal chores or showing up for their children's bedtimes. The upside of Sagittarius' unpredictability is that their usually sunny disposition makes them great company, and the minute the sun's up, they'll be on the lookout to make the best use of the day – inviting everyone along for the ride.

Any sort of living arrangement with Sagittarius involves a fair amount of compromise, and the trick is to find which sort of compromise they are willing to make. Attempts to subtly bring Sagittarius to heel often fail but what is easy with Sagittarius is open discussion. It may drive a partner or housemate mad to have to constantly ask for things to be done, but it is usually the only way, as Sagittarius is likely to be oblivious to putting the rubbish out, unless asked to do it.

Breaking up
with Sagittarius

Sagittarius may think it's OK to gallop off into the sunset with just a metaphorical flick of the tail in farewell when they break up with a lover, but this is often done in defence, irrespective of whether they are the one leaving or being left. And while this fits well with a reputation Sagittarius has for being footloose and fancy free, it can speak volumes about how they deal with heartache: by ignoring it. Given that each relationship is the opportunity for a new adventure, though, they are pretty resilient and will soon be looking for pastures new, although that's not to say they don't care. What they do expect, however, is to be able to stay friends, and in this they are straightforward – and surprised if their ex doesn't feel the same.

Sagittarius and . . .

Sagittarius

♈ Aries

Intellectually, physically and with a wide range of shared interests, these two are well suited in numerous ways. Sagittarius' more philosophical approach can sometimes irritate Aries and they both have strong views and tempers – but the sex is hot, too!

♋ Cancer

Sagittarius' freestyle approach to love plays havoc with Cancer's need for security, although the sensuality of the crab is initially intriguing. It's not enough, though, to compensate and keep each other interested, but a friendship could endure.

♉ Taurus

Taurus has a need to control that won't sit comfortably with Sagittarius, although the bull's earthy nature can initially attract. In the long term, Sagittarius needs independence and spontaneous fun, which might derail this pairing.

♌ Leo

Lots to chime here: with an equal love of adventure, socialising and freedom, there's little conflict about how to spend their time, while Sagittarius' light-hearted approach doesn't clash with Leo's tendency to be rather grand. Happy times.

♊ Gemini

There's a spark of immediate recognition between these two, who share a bright wit and imaginative approach to love, proving to be lots of fun both in and out of the bedroom. Even if it doesn't last, it'll be good while it did and amicable on parting.

♍ Virgo

Lots of interesting conversations to be had on a cerebral level but not much else, and overall Sagittarius tends to find Virgo's need for organisation and attention to detail creates too small a canvas for their freewheeling taste.

♎ Libra

There's an unexpected harmony between these two, because Libra adapts easily to Sagittarius' need to explore and offers luxurious opportunities in which to do so, while also balancing an emotional need for freedom.

♑ Capricorn

Sagittarius' compulsively social side is a mystery to Capricorn, who's a bit of a loner and expects a committed relationship from the word go. Both have high expectations, but these tend to play out too differently to be very compatible.

♏ Scorpio

Possessive, intense Scorpio may intrigue Sagittarius and seduce them physically at first, but it's all a bit much and it won't be long before Sagittarius' instinct to run away from the endless confrontations kicks in. Tricky from the word go.

♒ Aquarius

Prospects for this pair are good because they each have a highly imaginative, creative and outgoing side, and won't try to tie each other down. Commitment might take a while, but the slow burn can be a real turn on.

♐ Sagittarius

The connection between two like signs can bring out the best in each other – or the worst. While a love of freedom is all very well, they do need to be travelling in the same direction to even get to first base, so may end up more like siblings than soul mates.

♓ Pisces

That fiery energy is very attractive to dreamy Pisces, who finds Sagittarius' exploratory nature exciting. In the end, however, Sagittarius finds all that emotion too restrictive and can come to resent the drain on their freedom.

Sagittarius love-o-meter

Least compatible

Scorpio Capricorn Cancer Pisces Taurus Virgo

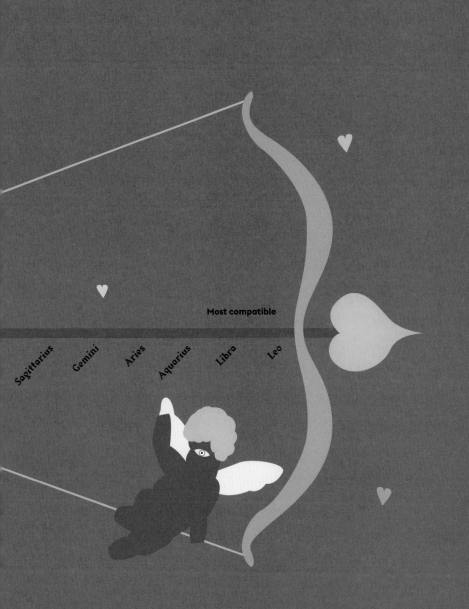

Most compatible

Sagittarius   Gemini   Aries   Aquarius   Libra   Leo

Capricorn

*

The goat

22 DECEMBER–20 JANUARY

Ruled by Saturn, Capricorn is
a cardinal earth sign associated
with hard work and depicted by the
sure-footed and sometimes playful
goat. Trustworthy and unafraid of
commitment, Capricorn is often very
self-sufficient and has the discipline
for the freelance working life.

OPPOSITE SIGN

Cancer

How does Capricorn want to be loved?

Feeling secure is an important part of how Capricorn wants to be loved. It's not that they are needy types, far from it, but Capricorn's emotional self-reliance is also something of a defence against time wasting, which only feeling secure can overcome. It takes a smart suitor to see that any emotional reserve can be part of their sizing up process, and only when they are 100 per cent sure of whoever's courting them will that person be rewarded with a show of interest.

Contrary to outward appearance, Capricorn is also a sign that likes to be pursued in the classically romantic way – red roses, anyone? – only it has to be authentic. Capricorn is very canny about other people's motivations, and it may feel a bit as if someone has to prove themselves time and time again. Capricorn always looks to the future and plans for it, so they want to be loved by someone who has a similar view of a shared future. Given their private natures, it's only by paying close attention that it will be possible to work out how Capricorn wants to be loved.

There's a balance to be struck, however, because Capricorn is also – like other earth signs – sensual and very much aware of physical pleasure, which they relish. They recognise that it's often a way in which it's possible to get to know someone else, and they can be quite realistic about this, too. Physical love is a direct expression of mental love for many Capricorns, and this earthy side can sometimes surprise, given their tendency towards caution. You can bet your bottom dollar, however, that any move is only ever made after carefully judging a situation. And once they commit, it's total and unlikely to wane.

What flowers should you buy Capricorn?

The carnation, with its long life, and pansies.
that reflect Capricorn's thoughtful nature,
are both flowers sure to delight Capricorn.

What is Capricorn like in bed?

Capricorns tend to be earthy sensualists with a strong sex drive. They are generally happy in their bodies and like to express love with an almost poetic physicality. Not for them a hasty experience in a hay field, they want to take their time in comfort and warmth and soft lighting. It's not luxury so much that Capricorn is after, but to feel secure enough to express themselves and this may take a certain amount of forethought and planning. It may sound contradictory but, for Capricorn, being spontaneous in bed takes thought and time.

Sexual fidelity is often the rule with Capricorn; once committed they're loyal and can be quite conservative on this front. And although a Capricorn likes to be talked into bed – mental stimulation is important – once they've decided to get down to it, they won't want to waste time talking further. That said, once comfortable and secure they're not afraid to say what they like and what they want from their lover. And Capricorn looks for a recognisably equal lover who is as accomplished and self-confident as they are themselves. All this may sound rather exacting, which is a Capricorn trait, but once securely attached all this loosens up in a beautiful way.

Moving in
with Capricorn

As long as you are similarly inclined – that is, generally quite reserved, well organised and tidy – then living with Capricorn is pretty simple. Clashes can occur, however, when Capricorn comes home after another long day to discover that the dishwasher hasn't been stacked properly or that the laundry pile is tottering in the corner. It seems so simple to Capricorn to stay on top of things that they can never fathom why anyone would do it differently.

As long as they're not working on a deadline and the washing up's been done, Capricorn can be relatively relaxed company. They're genuinely social and like having people around, and don't often feel the need to disappear off on their own to recharge their batteries. Planning is key, as they are generous hosts and prefer to make sure everything is just right for their guests, rather than take pot luck, so anyone attempting a spontaneous visit may raise a quizzical Capricorn eyebrow.

Breaking up
with Capricorn

A pragmatist with a strongly practical streak, Capricorn can often appear rather a cool customer if their relationship breaks up. Whether or not they've instigated it, they tend to take a practical approach: it wasn't working, so best to move on and – this is very Capricorn – least said, soonest mended. No hard feelings. The trouble is, having made a deep commitment in order to have a relationship in the first place, it probably cuts deeper than it appears to resilient Capricorn. Their ex might think from their behaviour that there's no residual feelings to honour, but it won't be true. Having loved and lost (for whatever reason), Capricorn finds it takes time to recover. Not for them the rebound romance, and this is how an ex will know how much they once mattered.

Capricorn and . . .

♈

Aries

Aries' impulsive nature is a problem for many Capricorns, who need to take time over decisions and may find it difficult to believe that commitment from this outgoing fire sign is even possible. Often great friends, though, as both share ambition.

♋

Cancer

Zodiac opposites, there are complementary features, but also a chasm between Cancer's need for security and Capricorn's, which is more to do with bricks and mortar. There's a strong sexual attraction, but after that, all bets are off!

♉

Taurus

Two sensual earthy signs with a lot in common, both value their security and relish creating a home. Both also admire each other's strengths, while Taurus' affectionate stability helps overcome Capricorn's caution, allowing passion to flourish.

♌

Leo

Even if there's an initial attraction, Capricorn can't really understand Leo's exuberance and egotism, and the daily dose of adoration the lion needs is a demand too far for the reserved, discriminating goat.

♊

Gemini

Once the initial attraction has passed, there can be a problem. Gemini's excitable extravagance will try Capricorn's conservative patience on just about every front, while their airy verbal wit can make this earth sign feel a tad stodgy and inadequate.

♍

Virgo

Each is appreciative of the other's organised approach, their intellectual style and capacity for working hard, making this a harmonious coupling. It's only that, with so much reticence on both sides, the relationship could stagnate.

Libra

Libra's artistic appreciation, love of luxury and work/life balance can initially attract Capricorn, but over time there's a clash about responsibility and discipline and the earth sign's jealousy doesn't help either.

Capricorn

Compatible on almost all fronts – from attitudes to work, socialising and even money – there's full-on mutual appreciation that bodes well in the bedroom, too. But the possible flaw is that there's a tendency for life to be a bit dull.

Scorpio

This is a surprisingly good match given they're both so strong willed, but Capricorn's need for security is well met by Scorpio's possessiveness, which provides a powerful bond. And if their tempers clash and the sparks fly, it also fuels their romance.

Aquarius

Aquarius' unpredictable style unnerves Capricorn, who prefers organisation and schedules, and this irritates Aquarius. However, underneath all this is an appreciation of their very different qualities, which can make them friends if not lovers.

Sagittarius

Sagittarius' optimism is wonderfully invigorating to Capricorn's reserve, encouraging a lighter view of life, but in time this could begin to feel undermining, as if they're not being taken seriously – which Sagittarius won't understand.

Pisces

A lovely union: Capricorn finds Pisces' imagination enhances their dreams, while their ability to graft fuels a mutual commitment. Pisces' affectionate nature makes Capricorn feel secure, and this works well in the bedroom, too.

Capricorn love-o-meter

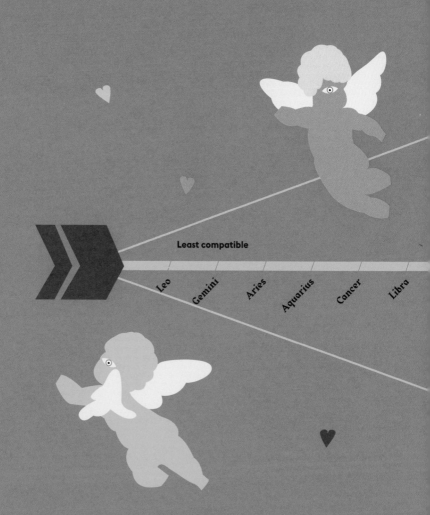

Least compatible

Leo   Gemini   Aries   Aquarius   Cancer   Libra

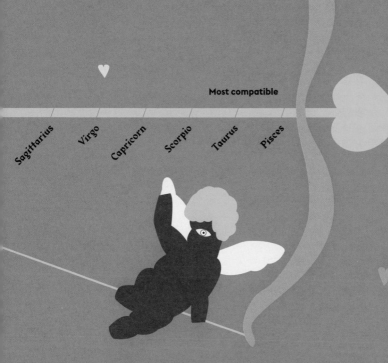

Most compatible

Sagittarius Virgo Capricorn Scorpio Taurus Pisces

Aquarius

*

The water carrier

21 JANUARY–19 FEBRUARY

Confusingly, given its depiction by the water carrier, Aquarius is a fixed air sign ruled by the unpredictable Uranus, sweeping away old ideas with innovative thinking. Tolerant, open-minded and all about humanity, its vision is social with a conscience.

OPPOSITE SIGN

Leo

How does Aquarius want to be loved?

The simplest answer to this question might appear to be: at a distance. There's a cool, reserved aspect to Aquarius' emotions that can give off quite a detached vibe, making it tricky for those who care deeply about them to work out how best to get close. Over-attention smacks of claustrophobia to Aquarius, and their dislike of this can be misinterpreted, so any loving has to acknowledge their independent nature. Labelling Aquarius as a commitment-phobe wouldn't necessarily be accurate: although their behaviour can often look like it, it could be a mistake to take it at face value. Communication, which is Aquarius' main suit, can be helpful here and they appreciate a straightforward approach.

If those trying to romance Aquarius find their behaviour perplexing, Aquarius is also perplexed when their relationships are problematic, because they – of course – perceive themselves as entirely straightforward. They want someone to love them who is as independent as they are, but available. An active disposition is great, but make sure that activity is as much in the mind as the body.

Shared interests are always a good place to start. In fact, partnerships with Aquarius are often forged over a joint project that stimulates mental activity. This allows shyer (yes, they do exist!) Aquarians to find their feet and learn to trust that their unconventional way of loving won't be rejected. Because often Aquarius can feel a little insecure and it's only over time that they will commit. When Aquarius makes a promise, they are likely to honour it. They are generous and tolerant and happy to build a future with someone who sparks their mind as well as their body.

What pet should you get with Aquarius?

As might be expected with an air sign, a bird is an attractive pet to consider buying with Aquarius. Because of their sociability, an electric blue-coloured love bird or two, or an exotic, talking Mynah bird might just fit the bill.

What is Aquarius like in bed?

Remember all those adjectives applied to Aquarius like unpredictable, experimental and unconventional? Yup, they apply here in the bedroom, too, and there's no doubt that for Aquarius, sex can be an intense, exciting and passionate affair – and even at times a little kinky. But here's the paradox, Aquarius can also be rather serious and thoughtful about things and although once they're in bed they're seldom cautious, it can take them a while to get there. There's nothing overtly flirtatious about Aquarius' sexual style. In fact, their sex life often starts in their head, because the primary stimulation for Aquarius can be somewhat intellectual, taking quite a while to reach the physical.

The one-night stand is unusual for Aquarius, as they prefer to get to know their lover's mind first. To their lover, this can look like the slow burn of caution, but it is usually more to do with Aquarius' tendency to focus on the individual they wish to get to know. Despite initial appearences, they are by no means a conventional lover. Once involved, Aquarius may surprise their lover with highly erotic talk as part of their repertoire and they might also suggest role play, new sexual positions and unusual locations.

Moving in
with Aquarius

'Live and let live' could have been a motto written by Aquarius and, for them, these words lie at the heart of their attitude when it comes to co-habiting. It's also the attitude they expect from their housemates, which might cause a little friction if you are not on the same page.

Aquarius is often away, either working long hours or just travelling for pleasure in some far-flung place. As a result they are used to fending for themselves and getting on with all sorts of different people. The upside to this is that they are generally very tolerant and open to discussion, so household problems are easily aired and solved. When they are around, Aquarians are very social, either spending hours at the kitchen table discussing the ways of the world with their lover or inviting a motley crew over to do the same.

Domesticity may be approached in a rather whirlwind way or methodically: Aquarius is too unpredictable to be sure. They may need the occasional prompt, but it will get done because at heart Aquarius does likes a degree of order and organisation.

Breaking up
with Aquarius

Aquarius doesn't much like the emotional extremes – their own or their ex's – that tend to occur with a break-up and will often continue with a relationship long after it's over (or wait until their lover does the breaking-up) in order to avoid potential heartbreak. Their response can be unpredictable, but their humanitarian heart means that they never enjoy hurting others and they also resent the sheer time and emotional energy it takes for the heart to heal. This also explains why Aquarius is often slow to commit, preferring to be friends for a long time before declaring their love in the first place. What Aquarius also expects is that they can be friends afterwards, once the dust has settled, and that's not always easy for an ex to tolerate, regardless of who called it off.

Aquarius and . . .

Aquarius

Aries

There's a mutual independence and spontaneity that makes this pair well matched on several fronts, meaning there's often plenty to be shared and enjoyed. But Aries' fiery dominance can sometimes prove a tad overbearing for Aquarius' need for freedom.

Cancer

Cancer's security is rooted in domesticity while Aquarius hardly notices their home surroundings, keen as they are to head off on their next adventure; and this disparity lies at the root of any trouble between these two. Not an easy match.

Taurus

Earthy, home-loving Taurus tends to find Aquarius' airy independence challenges their possessive side, fuelling anxious thoughts in both. There's also a difference of opinion about the water bearer's all-embracing humanitarian instincts.

Leo

High-spirited and adventurous, they both desire freedom but this can take different routes: Leo's through luxury and an audience while Aquarius wants an equal companion who can rough it when necessary. In this way their opposite natures can clash.

Gemini

These two air signs are well matched, both keen to live harmoniously and able to tolerate each other's need for freedom. Conversation is a huge part of their relationship and they can talk about just about everything with each other.

Virgo

Both recognise that they are as equally engaged with the mind as the body, but their goals tend to differ, with Aquarius aiming for innovative ideas and Virgo opting for more practical ones, which tends to knock out any compatibility of intellect.

Libra

This pair really know how to enjoy each other and easily spark each other's appetite for fun. While diplomatic Libra has no problem with Aquarius' stubborn streak, they may never quite manage to stabilise their relationship into anything other than a flirtation.

Scorpio

There's a strong attraction here but the unpredictability of Aquarius' nature can seriously chafe at Scorpio's intense needs and powerful passions, which Aquarius can find too much. They need to handle each other with care.

Sagittarius

There's an easy harmony between these two independent souls; neither is particularly jealous and both are inventive enough to hold each other's interest in the bedroom, which is where they are happy to reconnect after time spent apart.

Capricorn

Capricorn's cautious nature tends to bristle at Aquarius' airy disregard for the more practical side of life, while there's probably not enough of a sexual spark between them to offset Aquarius' boredom and get further than first base.

Aquarius

So comfortable will they be with each other, matched in interest for the new and the unusual, that they could only be happy together. The only downside is that they might not actually spend enough time together to cement any sort of lasting relationship.

Pisces

In spite of the real attraction here, Pisces' dreamy, spiritual side probably needs more harnessing in the real world than Aquarius can provide, which might make it difficult for this relationship to last without compromises on both sides.

Aquarius

Aquarius love-o-meter

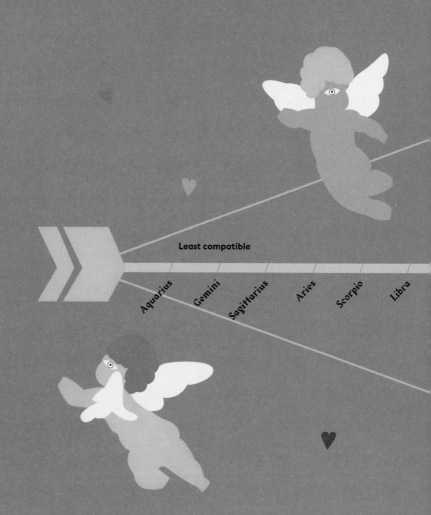

Least compatible

Aquarius Gemini Sagittarius Aries Scorpio Libra

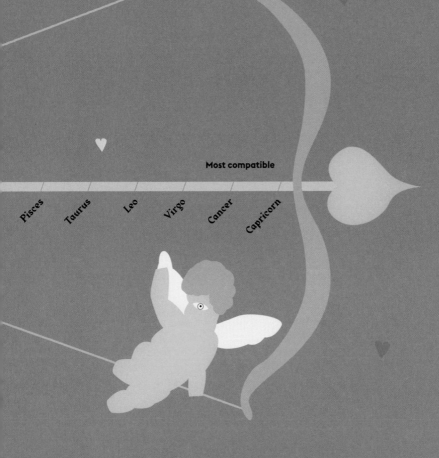

Most compatible

Pisces   Taurus   Leo   Virgo   Cancer   Capricorn

Pisces

*

The fish

20 FEBRUARY–20 MARCH

Acutely responsive to its surroundings, Pisces is a mutable water sign depicted by two fish, swimming in opposite directions, sometimes confusing fantasy with reality. Ruled by Neptune, its world is fluid, imaginative and empathetic, often picking up on the moods of others.

OPPOSITE SIGN

Virgo

How does Pisces
want to be loved?

Affectionate, romantic and sometimes a tad mystical when it comes
to loving, this is also pretty much how Pisces wants to be loved in
return, too. This is the sign most likely to believe in love at first
sight, soul mates and the sheer transcendence of spiritual union.
On the other hand, all of this can be brought down to earth with a
bit of a bump as reality bites and that unicorn disappears off into
the sunset. No matter, Pisces can generate love enough for two
and is soon off on another romantic quest.

Often Pisces also needs to feel needed, which can create a
tendency to gravitate towards emotionally needy people, who
may not be capable of loving Pisces quite enough in return. If this
happens, there's often an imbalance, which can be problematic.
It's important not to be blinded by the mere look of love and for
Pisces to keep one foot on the floor until they know for sure.

Pisces also needs to be loved by someone who isn't thrown
by their more sensitive reactions to the world, someone who can
reassure and ground them in the security of a more realistic and
enduring love. Forget 'treat them mean to keep them keen' as this
will just alienate tender-hearted Pisces, whose ego can't be
bothered with that sort of game playing. They are very much
an all-or-nothing type.

Ultimately, as long as they remember to keep some sort of grip
on reality and not let their heart rule their head completely, Pisces
can be happy in love. They must remember not to use love as a
manufactured opportunity for escapism from real life, however,
but learn to recognise the 'real thing', which will last.

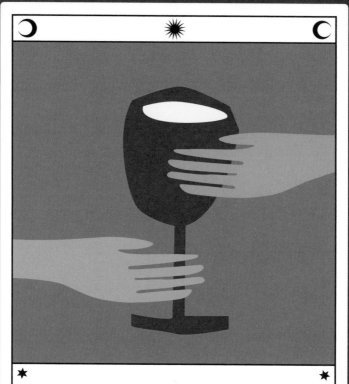

What colour should you wear on a date with Pisces?

As might be expected, the turquoise blue-greens of the ever-changing light and dark of the sea are Pisces' lucky colours. Wear these colours when you want to connect with Pisces energy. If you don't want to commit head-to-toe, choose blue or green for accessories – shoes, gloves, socks or even underwear.

What is Pisces like in bed?

Pisces' imagination can really run riot in the bedroom, and they are amongst the most sensuous and tactile of lovers – often more than happy to share the secrets of the shag. As long as they feel committed and secure, they're happy to plumb the ocean's depths. Tantric sex? Role play? Long, languid afternoon sex? In the bath or shower? At the beach? It's all possible as far as Pisces is concerned because they are all about expressing their feelings through the sensitivity of the body, understanding sex as an extension of a psychological connection. For Pisces, the two aspects of body and mind are almost one and the same when it comes to making love.

There can be a playfulness, too, as Pisces is usually blessed with a youthful inclination, whatever their age. As long as they're not trying to bury any uncomfortable feelings or using sex as escapism, Pisces can be a light-hearted, fun lover as often as they are intense; a lover who likes to confer pleasure as much as receive it. In many ways, they can be one of the easiest and most liberated of lovers, but not for someone in a hurry. Sex with Pisces is usually an imaginative three-course meal, not a snack.

Moving in
with Pisces

Pisces can make a captivating housemate because their natural affection, playfulness and sensitivity makes them very attuned to those around them. This makes them amongst the most thoughtful of people to live with, except when they disappear into a world of their own. Then, practical considerations of domesticity in particular can take a back seat while Pisces is preoccupied with whatever project or idea (or obsession) is currently occupying their imagination and creative mind. But Pisces are responsive people, too, so it only takes a little nudge to remind them of their responsibility to those they live with and, once reminded, they will gladly drop everything to do their bit.

It's a rare Pisces that chooses to live completely alone; they are not the hermits of the zodiac and prefer company. Pisces like to host visitors, too, to whom they offer anything from a meal to a bed for the night to an extended visit – sometimes without checking with their partner first.

Breaking up
with Pisces

There's a very private, not to say secretive side to Pisces, who can become extremely elusive when hurt, retiring to deep contemplation of a failed relationship or of their ex, regardless of who has done the breaking-up. Pisces is usually hopeless about asking for emotional support or help at this time, but needs to be realistic and not carry a torch for a lost love. Pisces hates hurting others and feels things so keenly that they have a tendency to feel the other person's pain almost as much as their own. This can become overwhelming, causing them to react by withdrawing from society, or into other forms of escapism, taking a while to recover. In this way, there's a tendency for Pisces to indulge their sorrow rather than confronting it and taking more positive steps to manage it.

Pisces

Pisces and . . .

♈︎

Aries

Unlikely as it might initially seem, there's a complementary link between Pisces' dreamy nature and need for security and Aries' more dynamic and assured approach to life that can work quite well between these two, as long as some tact is applied.

♉︎

Taurus

Taurus' extreme practicality is wonderfully useful in helping to realise the scope of Pisces' vision, but can sometimes be a little too heavy-handed for such a romantic, even though their mutual taste for creature comforts is well shared.

♊︎

Gemini

Both quick-witted by nature, there's an immediate attraction but one that is unlikely to be sustained given Pisces' dislike of Gemini's airy thoughtlessness, while Gemini tends to find Pisces' need for emotional reassurance impossible to fathom.

♋︎

Cancer

Both equally emotional and sensitive, Cancer has the edge on practicality, which helps balance this pairing and keep what could be rather a too-fluid relationship, stable. Once committed they are loyal to each other, although it might take them a while to settle.

♌︎

Leo

Tricky this one: Leo can't understand Pisces' dreamy hesitancy and tends to stomp all over their finer feelings. In turn, Pisces doesn't understand Leo's need for acknowledgement and admiration and also hates the lion's endless need to socialise.

♍︎

Virgo

Astrological opposites can complement each other well, but Virgo's extremely fastidious mind can find Pisces' inclination to prioritise dreams over reality completely maddening. There's unlikely to be enough romance, either, between these two.

♎

Libra

There can be an initial harmony between these two, because both like the artistic side of life and share a vision of what's beautiful, but Pisces' need for security is at odds with Libra's desire for freedom, which might undermine them in the end.

 ♑

Capricorn

An example of opposites attracting, these two are really well matched because Pisces relishes Capricorn's passion, strength of character and can-do attitude, while Capricorn loves Pisces' affectionate nature and romanticism.

 ♏

Scorpio

There's an immediate closeness between these two potentially intense water signs, where Scorpio's possessiveness actually helps Pisces feel loved rather than smothered, and they are equally sensual and imaginative with a strong sexual bond.

 ♒

Aquarius

Innovative Aquarius seems a perfect match for Pisces' idealism but there's too much airy detachment there to fully engage with Pisces' emotional approach. Plus, Aquarius' need for external stimulation frustrates Pisces' need for intimacy.

 ♓

Pisces

♐

Sagittarius

The problem here is Sagittarius' need for independence and activity outside the home, which Pisces finds very undermining. This restlessness feels like rejection to Pisces, while Pisces' dreamy romanticism irritates Sagittarius in turn.

♓

Pisces

There's probably too much sharing of a good thing here – sensitivity, romance, empathy, dreams and ideas – to make this relationship work well in real life. All this emotional fluidity could overwhelm them both, leading to an unhelpful interdependence.

Pisces love-o-meter

Least compatible

Leo   Virgo   Aquarius   Sagittarius   Pisces   Gemini

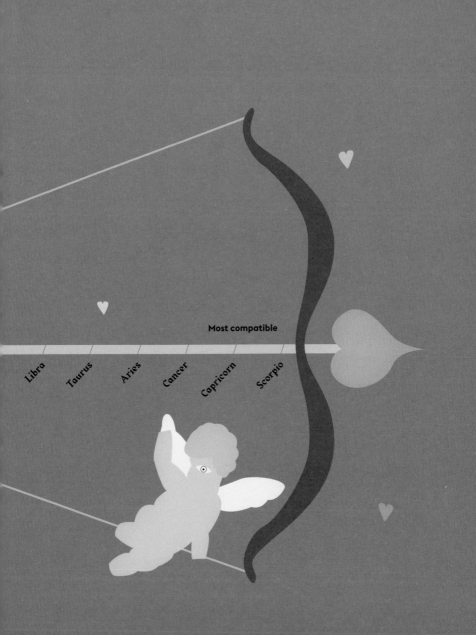

Most compatible

Libra Taurus Aries Cancer Capricorn Scorpio

About the author

Stella Andromeda has been studying astrology for over 30 years, believing that a knowledge of the constellations of the skies and their potential for psychological interpretation can be a useful tool. This extension of her study into book form makes modern insights about the ancient wisdom of the stars easily accessible, sharing her passion that reflection and self-knowledge only empowers us in life. With her sun in Taurus, Aquarius ascendant and moon in Cancer, she utilises earth, air and water to inspire her own astrological journey.

Published in 2019 by Hardie Grant Books, an imprint of Hardie Grant Publishing

Hardie Grant Books (London)
5th & 6th Floors
52–54 Southwark Street
London, SE1 1UN

Hardie Grant Books (Melbourne)
Building 1, 658 Church Street
Richmond, Victoria 3121

hardiegrantbooks.com

British Library Cataloguing-in-Publication Data.
A catalogue record for this book is available from the British Library.

Love Match
ISBN: 9781784883287

10 9 8 7 6 5 4 3

Publishing Director: Kate Pollard
Junior Editor: Bex Fitzsimons
Art Direction and Illustrations: Evi O. Studio
Editor: Wendy Hobson
Proofreader: Kay Delves

Colour reproduction by p2d
Printed and bound in China by Leo Paper Products Ltd.